ISBN: 9798334902695

For Lidia, always.

Contents

Is there a repellent rooted deep within my core?

The fall is inevitable, I am unravelling, my flower petals are withering, dying.

I sense the ground trembling beneath me but I dare not look down.

<u>*Descent into Chaos*</u>

A shipwreck shall come, the air is tinged with the salt of a storm. I know it, I am sorry. We shall be displaced from this soil, the sun is long gone.

Please, hold on, and do not let go until all of this is done.

Honey

Lie.

An art you have mastered,

sinking teeth into skin,

so firm you are

in your false-God convictions.

You, like a bee trapping me

into sticky, sickly honey.

Wings glued together,

unable to flee from the pool of deception

your fingertips have so carefully weaved.

But do I even wish to leave?

When a candy-drizzled fantasy

is so much more pleasant to the ears

than the deafening shrieks of reality?

I am stuck,

knee deep in verbal poison.

I grin and bear it all,

never speaking out.

Compelled to be silent.

Blind, compliant,

forgetting how to see past baseless promises.

Trapped,

but this too, is my very own doing.

3

Different

The air shifts, the magnolia seeds split open, fleshy coating. Slipping grip, *falling*, past the boundaries of an ignorant adolescence and the limb-cracking weight of adulthood (you carved a promise into tree bark that we need not grow up, and yet). Soft hands declined, innocence dwindling, dissipating, crimson petal on white, a frightful sort of metamorphosis (butterfly to caterpillar, reverse), a wretched new becoming.

Leaving, loss.

A first encounter with **abandonment**. Remember this word, for it shall grow to become everyone's second name as the familiar decays away.

Change is never a good thing, no matter what anyone tells you. Everyone is hardwired to leave in the end.

Reckless

Sunlight seeping in through the cracks, giddy and feverish once. Mulberries calling to be ripped apart from leaves. Dripping crimson-stained strawberries, guilty, *leaking* fingertips, kingfishers mocking such deceit, poison, poison ivy hedges. Tremors of the sun, trees sprouting from the roots of prehistoric sentiments. Delirious from all this vibrancy, this life to seize and snatch.

Perhaps this very desire was our downfall to begin with.

Devouring like thieves, robbers, existing on borrowed time, racing, a portal to the other world. The bitter months shall soon commence, seeking to punish the reckless and wild who exploit the fruits of the earth for self-gain. This summer, however, I shivered at the sight of all the possibilities.

Sunflower

Cast me away from the light,

I thrive in pure darkness now.

Heliotropism no longer sustains,

I do not tilt eastwards

to track the sun's face.

A *fall* from grace,

a bow in reverence,

an admitting of the weakness.

For autumn is approaching,

and already I mourn

the loss of the heavenly gold,

withering, shedding skin

in a manner helpless, faithless.

I cling onto glory that no longer feeds,

I do not wish to feel,

I am carried by the wind,

and softened by the leaves

that do not succeed in diluting my grief.

grief is something you can dilute?

Descent

The sun sets,

the weeds clog the ecosystem of my arteries.

I inch closer but you retreat,

I mourn the substantial loss of your angel wings.

Farewell kiss, soil uncoiled,

a descent into chaos,

birthing seeds that are fated to be wretched.

Grazing knees, reddening clay,

bargaining with God to obey,

a saviour to eliminate decay,

the wilting, the shrivelling up of unholy plants.

Is it so strange to believe that the soul was not destined to stray far from the body?

Fluid is in short supply.

Greenhouse,

but I blare red, my petals unfed,

the sunlight that once glittered

in between curtain coils dead.

The rot seeps into carpet fibres

like the unfiltered laughter of a once happy home.

The undergrowth does not relent so easily.

Actor

The curtain falls,

mask down,

echoes of the applause make me feel

dizzy

might drown

in the depth of the day's pretending.

Never ending, the curtain call,

but how else might I find meaning

in the metaphors?

Cold relentless heart,

callous, cracked,

the perfect act

(who am I without these tragic lines

philosophized?)

I frantically flip through the script,

trying to recall

if I remembered my lines today

Or did I forget all my lies today?

Moon

When I catch myself

believing that you are sorry for your mistakes,

following after me rapidly

to express your regret,

I think of how the moon looks

as if it is stalking you

while actually staying in the same place.

OMG.

Perspective

Cursing your name and pushing you far, far away. Pessimistic, masochist. Cynic – what is in it for you, what is behind all this devoted attentiveness toward me? Feigning love for a soul overflowing with decaying matter.

Surely there is a hidden agenda I have failed to decipher.

Avoiding eye contact. Hurling words that are like targets programmed to hit right where it hurts. A bullet, salt to the wound. I want to see my words land right where they will evoke sheer pain, witness my actions affect you for once. But this, all of this behaviour, is not really so much anger as it is *pleading*, to remain in your faith despite the tantrums, despite the difficulty to obstacle course your way through my interior.

Testing your boundaries, experimentation. How tough are you really, how far are you willing to go, to tolerate for me?

How long until I break you just the same too?

(I cannot save myself, and neither can you).

Autumn

Is there a sort of magic

that lies in the gentle dance of the leaves?

The faint but melodic whispers of the wind

spilling the secrets of the earth inside of your ear?

The hues of the sky are auburn

and the world is on fire

Before everything dies, it comes alive.

Tea

Porcelain goods, fumes of cinnamon tea, disrupting, **erupting**, accumulation of sin, sieving the leaves, watching as you leave, I am vindicated by each slam of the door, marking your betrayal of the metaphor (to remain for all of eternity), inconstancy a revered flavour, this fragile tainted heartbeat, the clock on the mantelpiece, *ticks*, I am always right where you left me, I have not been anything other than 15 since. I stir your tea, I mix the neurons of your mind, what lies in the depths of all you contrive, you never liked to arrive, to depart was your preferred method of displaying affection, farewell, goodbye (please never come back, I loathe you more than anything in my entire life) (I am still stirring your tea, my fingertips shriek for reprieve).

Extinguished

Dried flowers // in love notes // teeming with // false feelings // the right combination of words // can make one forget // they are grieving // over people of the past // childhood phantoms // golden days turned rust // when you were not tainted by all those lies // writing dead poetry // parchment soaked in ink // always useless apologies // mourning your indifference // the person you were // in my head // deep in the soils of my imaginings

Anxiety

Anxiety is a merciless sort of misery.

I am unable to decipher whether my agitations of the future are exaggerated or eerily realistic. Whether the slight indentation in his eyebrow signals anger or whether it is all a figment of my imagination. What is real and what could never be.

And so I spend ninety nine percent of my time worried about scenarios that cease to happen. Everything is alright in the end, it always is. But in the beginning, at the very start of something daunting, my brain fails to process that THE TIGHTNESS IN MY CHEST WILL UNFOLD. Have a little faith. I should have a little *faith*.

Yearning

When the soil has basked in enough sunlight,

it beckons for the rain to fall,

yearning for drops of fluid against

the parched, grainy ground,

a ravenous craving for the sky's tears,

unable to cope with the foreignness of light.

Ultraviolet hues of florets shun the sun,

receptive only to cloudbursts,

painful pelting drizzle.

When flowers are in the sunlight for too long, they become damaged.

Oh, how afraid I am that this is human nature too.

When we grow weary of yellow-coated happiness,

we begin to seek change in blue-tinged sorrow.

When the sunlight caresses our skin for too long,

we ungratefully retreat to the shade.

Return

A brief flashback to the summer.

Fever stroke, the way the crimson of the fruit juice trickled down your throat. Childish indifference to stains, careless attitude toward the crimson tint that berries left on fingertips (that will take decades to polish off from the crevices of our skin). Magnetic attraction to scarlet and chaos, irrational passion, foolish vigour. Acting without desire for justification, selfish, claiming rights to whatever we like. But there must be law and order (we cannot be trusted to rely on moral code). Whatever we bite into we spoil, ruin, taint, infected apple, our own category of forbidden fruit. A naïve belief in the fact that our rotten deeds would fail to catch up to us.

Costume party

It is Halloween for me every day. I am always attending this costume party called life with a carefully-crafted mask. I am too far gone – I've no clue where the disguise ends and where I begin anymore. I am so accustomed to this role that I cannot quit the act. Because if I step outside of it and be myself, the curtains will fall and the audience will leave and the play will cease to be interesting.

(Does knowing me lead to loving me less?)

So come on, why don't you stay? I'll do some extra pretending for Act II, Scene V.

Jack-o'-lantern

Make a jack-o'-lantern out of my heart, right now. Overcome your biggest fear and behold the inside of me. Beware, the external beauty you believe I possess in no way mirrors the hidden parts deep within. Have you the courage to peer into my rotten soul, to extract all of the dreadfulness out? Carve into me a joyful face, in a way that allows the light to seep in through the cracks. Do not stop until you have finished, until the trace of every devastation is wiped out for eternity, until I am created anew from the power of your sculptor-like hands.

I desire to be restored. A treasure valuable enough to hold.

Leaves

The decaying of leaves,
the eve of searing fingertips.

Autumn lodges itself
between the ribcage bars of my heart –
prisoner, incision.

I paint my nails crimson,
I shed polish on heel-print walnut shells.

There is a sort of screaming
beneath the surface
of the changing weather,
a gradual spiral
into nothing pure,
into everything tempting.

Perhaps your hands

may offer me absolution.

Perhaps I may soften

the crinkling wrinkles

of my plastic-plastered smile

with your maple-tinged sight

(false prophet declarations).

I fake freckles with cinnamon dust.

I tug my turtleneck lower.

I grieve, I weep,

I consider transforming into a wild thing.

I consider transporting out of this skin.

I am a pit stop. A hotel but never a home.

You claim I mean the world to you but you behave as if I am a pit stop, a gas station to fuel you up for your final destination. A means to an end,

a placeholder,

until the one you really crave returns your useless affections.

I am a shadow, a   frag ment   of a whole.

Discarded after use, ~~damaged~~ goods. But you have already yanked off the price tag, receipt thrown out. It is not as simple as returning me, leaving.

I refuse to comply with consumer demands.

Skeletons

The skeletons and I converse, we are friends, closet residence, far behind hoarded clothes, five year old dolls. Cold tea in the kettle on the stove, sifting through a past I refuse to let go of. <u>Everything that was once lovely has long since decayed</u>, photograph edges *frayed*, purple-turned spines, hearts long flatlined. My mother did warn to not reside in the hearts of everchanging beings.

But if I shed the skin of years past, what ode to the golden days will outlast? What will my fingernails latch onto with a potency greater than tragic loves, what shall be left if not the discarded bones of those who used to be a home? How could my petals ever bloom again?

This tendency to latch onto deceased matter will surely be the death of me too.

You are a canvas of screaming colour and I am muted, diluted.

I am pastel, not cranberry red. I am hues that devastate.

Diluted Colours

Everything is stagnant.

I fast instead of feast, I fear the swallowing.

Changing

Icicle collision, desperate declarations of hope. An attempt to tame the lion, the one who will outmanoeuvre the fire. You wish to make a home out of me but I cannot be a warming hearth, only the chill polluting your bone marrow, your anxieties personified. Unpredictable as the waves crashing against the shore, tide ebbing and flowing (this getting older is inescapable now). Wind groaning, shadows humming under tree leaves. Machinations of grandeur and deceit, the very phantom you fail to outrun in your sleep (me).

When flowers get too much water, they cannot breathe. A damaged flower cannot be in direct sunlight, lest it get burnt. Its leaves are too sensitive for the light. After periods of blue, yellow will make it vulnerable. This is not poetic, but merely a simple fact.

Absence

The light is not the same these days. The daylight is bruised, its splendour diluted. Sunsets no longer scream in marmalade and saffron hues – the orange sleeps now, watered-down, exhausted. All love is void of passion, void of danger – scream at me, utter words that evoke indigo-shaded tears, vermilion anger. Say something, say anything, for I fear neutrality and indifference.

Everything is pale, lamppost light. The sun does not rise with the same vivacity, we do not absorb maple-tinged happiness in the same manner. Winter strips light of its goodness, of its vibrancy. Dreary grey, foggy skies mirroring my foggy mind. But the blue gets darker, a sort of unbearable sadness that drowns the world out. The daylight is bruised, the auroras battered. The soul inside me that lives on rays of violet shatters.

January

Strawberry juice

dripping

from our chins

lips   drenched   in   a

   sickly

sweetness

             impossible

to

CONTAIN

Our fingers are crimson-stained and we have
frequent flashbacks to summer, the golden days
when the world belonged to us, nothing out of
reach, ambitions exceeding our own good.

But let us not forget, winter lingers —

it is only January after all.

And so every bite is coated with a layer of frost, and the ice does not melt but rather hardens within us because there is a bitter chill that soaks through our veins and it cannot be broken, no, not until the sun rises once more.

Nothing to let go of, but nothing to latch onto.

Sceptical

I do not believe you // liar// pathological //
worship God // not people // false // love is a
myth // scam // payment declined // who
made this up // "love" // thought it up and ran
with it // convinced others to hold out for it //
LOVE IS A MYTH // fairytale // embellished
// glitter over the fading gold // not real life //
not on this earth // do not count on it // don't
// With love comes // the peeling back of //
multi-faceted layers // a glimpse into my measly
thoughts // more rot than girl // decay than life
// more fragile to break // sensitive to damage
// so I would rather // pretend // to be made
out of iron // unbreakable // nothing touches
her // nothing moves her // firm boulder //
heartless // but I like it that way // that is how
// to keep affection out // to keep everyone at
arm's length //

Cold/warm bones

Scarred by the fire, burning desire,

failure to be engulfed.

Taming, slicing this furious passion

into pieces,

becoming the ice,

consumer, consumption,

consoling is not holding.

Every inch of your body screams

red and orange hues,

deep burial of longing

six feet under,

shadows of shadows themselves,

tamer of flames,

unable to emerge unscathed.

Battalion scars, polluted angel wings,

cold hand to fevered forehead.

Sceptical of affection, protection.

Saviour of souls,

A futile hope to be resurrected whole.

Frosty

I freeze every little thing I touch, transform it into menacing attributions of frost. Snowstorms manifest within my veins, preserved by the constant flow of bitterness harboured along the very crevices of my soul.

Hard to love, not saffron and sunny but indigo and silver, minus temperatures. It is an igloo in here. Violet shades rather than the natural bright blush that comes from close contact with the fire. I simply exist, meander amidst sun-tinged individuals to get a dying glimpse (of light). I am not cold but I *am* the cold. I repel and I am glad of it.

Stagnant

Everything is stagnant and I try to make sense of it all. I am aware of the important and life-altering nature of a decision, hence why I am so indecisive. *I would be to blame I would be to blame* it would be my fault for making the wrong move, for catapulting my life and the lives of others into ruin. I like to be clever, to think things through, to be the best for myself and for my loved ones. I am not perfect but I hang onto my futile attempts to be.

Does God cry?

What I am asking is,

do the tough still break?

Do they internalise their armour

or crack under the pressure of it?

Do the purest souls

with wings of silk

still feel wretched and damned,

even though they have been redeemed?

Is an angel's fall fatal,

or is it simply a light grazing of the knees?

Are the empathetic ever exempt

from desiring to quit,

from ever praying for sturdy arms to fall into?

God gets tired of it too, unrequited love.

Shielding those who do not wish to take cover.

A chink in the armour,

a perfect opening

for someone, anyone, to heal.

Polluting my heart instead,

making it that much more difficult to breathe

(narrowing the fine lines of anatomy).

Tell me that for once I do not have to

possess this marble power.

Tell me that it is not pathetic to want to be

carried.

To carry

I am a chore,

hefty baggage, luggage,

so carelessly discarded.

Faulty core,

I give until my palms are quivering,

but when my hands are void of offering,

everybody scatters

(heart so shamelessly battered).

To be left, to be abandoned,

side street,

spine-cold concrete for a companion,

pavement for a friend,

apathetic armour to defend.

When could I be wanted for my soul?

What are the requirements to be kept?

What wire runs through my bones

that repulses in such a manner?

I hold on, I let go.

I abandon belief in the permanent.

I make peace with the fact

that everybody leaves.

Sweet

Sweet on the outside, but terrible and tangy within. You can handle bits of me, orange peels, but never the entire thing, never the sour core that makes your face twist and turn in bitterness. I must be something manageable, palatable, never too much, way too much in full form. My bright shades of orange you revere when it is amongst golden and maroon hues, like a sunset in the sky, or marigold flowers, but orange on its own, isolated, you find blinding. You sugarcoat me with everything beautiful, sprinkle me with cinnamon to conceal my muchness, to dilute my meagreness.

Sorry sorry sorry, I choke out.

I still make you sick.

OH SHIT.

46

Flower

Like a rotting flower

Unravelling

Petals f

      a

             l l i ng

apart by the minute

Sun reflecting on the other side

             of wherever I am

Stigma *cracking* slowly

All of my beauty *dissipating*

to reveal the rotten brown pistil,

the very nucleus that I attempt to shield.

One wound was enough.

Later, I vowed that no one

would ever peel back my layers,

my core now forever concealed.

Diminishing

And when you walk through the door,

passing me by as if I were invisible,

I do not tell you

that I had been looking through the window

all day, awaiting your arrival.

I swallow the shame of being too eager,

childlike excitement, deflated.

Yes, I have worshipped you,

stupid

(the Book does say that you should not have any

other gods before Him).

I cannot be so ignorant to think that the love others have for me will be constant.

oh...

Floater

Never a house, never a home. Light and free, soaring away from all the constraints of the Earth.

"Let us be birds," we used to say, when things became unbearable to cope with.

Untamed, wild. But what if I wish to be tamed after all? All I ever did was run. Liquid not solid, but how I wish there was actually some weight to me. To have someone to hold on to. I can only run so much, only fly so high. We humans were not made to imitate the wind. We humans were made for each other, out of each other. We were never meant to float like ghosts of pasts that will never and can never return. Born to be wanted, forced to be a floater. *Is it the greatest trial in the world to hold on?*

Uninteresting

Now my stream of thoughts and overthinking have become uninteresting and my devastation is no longer good company.

I am trying not to be someone people can dislike.

(but I think I am finally sick of pantomime acts and losing myself in the process)

Constancy

Constancy – myth, folktale, legend,

the atoms of abandonment

woven deep into your tapestry.

The slam of the door feels like a kiss,

the creaky hinges a victory

(you could not prove me wrong,

your leaving stirs a sort of birdsong

within the strings of my apathetic heart).

Who could have saved if not I,

homeless fingertips

against skin that is mine?

What could make you salivate

if not the saving grace of flora,

the rotten shade of mulberry hues?

Perhaps you might recall

the strawberry-seeded slide of the mouth,

the mingling of souls

within wide gaps of the earth,

perhaps you might regret.

Coffee <u>(TRIGGER WARNING: EDs)</u>

Coffee still stains the surface of my teeth, seeps into my gums, the black, the liquid void of milk. I grieve, the sweetness before the sin, the freedom before the free fall. I gnaw at granules trapped in gaps, the burnt taste on the tongue. I consume to shrink, to feel something, to feel nothing at all. The apples are sweeter when poison filled, red glimmer skin against sunshine, the naïve belief in the fact that I could ever be adored (rather abhorred). *I want to be attracted to anything other than tragedy.* I sink, I drink, the coffee cradles me whole, caresses my soul (I put the kettle on for more).

Rage

My rage rapidly translates into humiliation:

What do I have to say for myself?

Why do I envy the fully grown flowers

and what have become of my angel wings?

Snowdrop

Snowdrop, early riser.

Perhaps I emerged from the womb

preceding the earth's yearly thawing.

Petals plucked,

ruthless doings,

scratched against innocent skin surfaces

that had not yet known sin.

Hope amidst graveyards,

the deathly resonance of a plea

that echoes, unheard of

cloaked by the fog.

Mocked,

taunted by the sun that conceals itself

behind the swallows' hiding spot.

Quivering fingertips,

eyes darting across the wreckage,

desperate to salvage even the slightest survivor,

a sting of tears,

of hope futile,

unattainable,

(nothing to resurrect beneath the shadows of the
dead).

I bloomed too soon,
now I no longer try.

I sink into the soil

and vow to survive,

to heal the heart

that the camellias

so desired to crack.

Homesick

My dark and lonely

craves a companion,

its equivalent,

spitting image of a twin

that only resides in the hollow

of your bone marrow.

We bond over how

our white blood cells respond to affection

as a foreign parasite –

cancerous,

a thing that must be destroyed.

wow

This purple matter

flowing within veins

dominates.

Falsity, to me,

built on unreliability.

I cannot disprove the theory

that everyone relishes leaving.

Yet, my wide and silent corridor

seeks solace in your galaxies of despair,

before the apathy of our native language

was drilled into your skeletal system.

I am homesick for the very thing that led me to evacuate. We cannot save those too far gone, and yet I feel that familiar itch to play hero again.

Unbound

Do I wish to be unshackled from the groans of despair, bones under repair? What lies beyond the biting bindings of winter soil? Perhaps certain fractures are destined to remain cracked and kintsugi is a myth. Perhaps abandoning the bandage is the etiquette and the loneliness will caress like a kiss. Could I be acquainted with my soul once more, void of a gaping hole? Or shall I give up the ability to create such poetry? Desire spilling past the brim is what encompasses my very essence. The awareness of an unfavourable palette is in fact a reprieve from feeling sea-sick, a sort of overthinking until disease.

Prying

Intruder // invader // prodding poking // at
this shell of a heart // fumbling stumbling // for
a way in // lock and key // door hinges rusty //
from so many people // leaving // like it is easy
// maybe it is // maybe I should try it // uno
reverse // pull a you on you // on all of you //
see what it feels like // when the tables turn //
and the very core of your soul // *burns* // aches
// hope // a flickering flame // do not go out
// do not move // eyes bulging // keep your
eyes on the light // cling onto God not people
// people leave // never make a home out of
them // mortals // flawed beings // I am //
unreliable myself // I will admit // attention
deficit

Eye-opening

I used to believe that it is fine if I wallow in my sadness, but this mode of alleviating any worry can only last so long. Looking down at my hands and staring at the light flowing within the crevices of my palms, I could not simply let it escape me forever.

Regular

Everyone has changed // irrevocably //
undeniably // and I feel unusual // for staying the
same // yes I have grown // yes I have flourished
// the things I love // have come and gone //
but at my core // I remain unchanged // the way
I look at the moon // my morals // my desires //
will I forever be // endlessly // consistent //
constant // no element of surprise // regular?//

Mountains

Of mountains and hills. Of heights never too daunting to climb. Childhood heart beating erratically, fearless in the face of consequence (for treacherous actions). Unafraid of affection, desiring it.

But what is desire anyway? What can a little human being know about yearning, *wanting* something so badly that you cannot get out of bed?

Stepping on discarded snail shells, tugging flowers from out the soil, no inherent value for all things beautiful. Unaware of how long the pretty takes to cultivate. Did we grow up too fast? Did we scowl at the sun for so graciously pouring heat onto us when now it is the very thing that we crave, the very thing that we lack? *Sorry sorry sorry*. But why no second chance? Why a cruel, indifferent universe? Why absence of faith?

Foolish, sheltered kids, unaware of such a thing as tragedy (late acquaintance to the world's evils).

Forbidden fruit, sticky red apple dye on fingertips

(we were better off not knowing).

A wish to rewrite it all.

A wish only.

Hope and hesitation

Hesitation to hope

Hold on

Attach yourself to my soul

It is my insides that crave

Foolish, I am lying

Desire = laughable

I would rather isolate than beg

Comfort myself than swallow

The shame of asking

Why ask

We emerged from the womb alone

After all

Is connection necessary

Love is loss

And leaving

Always leaving

Better to never fall

Better to shield

Armour, steel

No chink, no crack

I spent years building this fortress

I shall not open up the gates for anyone.

↳ Iron
exterier;
flowers
inside.

A torch, a light in the dark –

The monsters were streetlight shadows

The thorns were flower roots

<u>Out of the Shadows</u>

From the mortar tunnels I emerge

Orange bleeding horizon –

A wound patched up, ordained

Spring

Eventually, we must make something beautiful out of this mess, the vapour of our lips fogging windowpane breath. Maybe seas do not always have to be something we must drown in. We can turn this ache into a sort of art, worthy of framing, of feeling.

We may never be able to seek a state of complete yellow but maybe we can meet happiness halfway. Merge our indigo with golden-tinged landscapes to form a midpoint, an evergreen forest, the breathtaking wonder of the rolling hills colliding with our best and worst parts.

Succulent star fruit. The dew that forms on grass after torrential rains. Emeralds glistening in the sun, a promise of a rainbow in the aftermath of storm wreckages.

We do not have to part with the blue within ourselves but we can simply make peace with it.

A truce, a deal with time, a shade of being that allows us to be terrifically miserable and devastatingly joyous all at once.

Reborn

Just lay with me on the grass. Twist a blade of it in between your fingertips, marvel at all the earthly colour that has been restored to this bleak universe. A glimpse of a potentially attainable paradise. Hold me in a way that does not make me flinch and banish all of my cynicism. Let us make snow angels in the spring, our testimony that we have been reborn.

Proof we did not let the cold define us.

Sharp

I am spiky thorns and metal daggers,

void of the captivating crimson of rose petals.

I am the sharp spikes of a lily's roots,

a dark contrast to its sinless white.

I am the anger bubbling underwater,

I am chaos and conflict

with a futile desire to be soft and harmless.

I am in the process of trying

aiming for *softer softer softer.*

Let yourself be held for once,

surrender your armour.

Fear

Anxious, clumsy, overthinker.

Constant need of water for my petals (without reassurance my stigma will crack). Every glance of yours tinged with even the faintest frown will be food for my fears. Perhaps I am destined to be the only one soaked through such tears, maximum sensitivity, a blinding desire to be desired, all of it futile.

Bloom

Despite it all,

we break through the soil,

shocked that we have bloomed,

shocked we have been born into bright colours.

Now, we are what the sun sings sopranos to.

All the light that has been hibernating rises

to find solace in the early bird's chirps.

We may never be detached from our roots,

but we grow taller.

Injustice

To me you were the villain,

I bathed in my naivety so graciously,

Ignoring your pleads to be understood.

But inevitably, I grew up,

and there you stood, suddenly a hero.

Please do not forget that despite my ignorance,

I never stopped loving you.

(Heroes do not flaunt or wear capes but they suffer,
make sacrifices for those they adore)

Thank you, sorry.

Tulip

Always the early riser,

never failing to be the first.

I can be every colour:

vibrant pink, yellow, and orange,

but never blue,

never a colour that would make you

discontented too.

And when I am hurt,

my petals and stems crack and break,

but I will continue to grow,

continue to stand tall,

and cease to display any sign of weakness.

I am tough to manage,

but beautiful nevertheless.

Possibilities

Momentarily,

the sun comes out of hiding,

and the branches bend in a gesture that

can be likened to a smile.

The gravel is golden,

the air mimics the fragrance of

something similar to hope,

and the Earth awakens from its slumber.

Now, goddesses are possible.

Love at first sight

You walk in // and my mouth has the urge to // fall wide open // you speak // but I do not acknowledge your voice // or rather // I pretend not to // although it reverberates through me // I look down at the floor // instead of into those eyes // because I know // I am certain // that in my transfixion I will be unable to look away // besides // I do not believe // in love // anyway

I do not sound so convinced.

No, but what of my philosophies?

Light

Who needs constellations when you exist in the same lifetime as I do? The stars envy those who are worthy enough to witness your brightness up close, a burning tapestry of enchantment across centuries. They are light years away from observing the cosmic collisions unfolding within the rims of your eyelids, they desire the juice that turns your blood flow golden. Not a single mortal on this earth has hands that can heal like yours, palms that can remedy even the most miserable heart. Such power is only recited in folktales, and yet here you are, living proof that humans can be saviours too. You are the lighthouse captains seek when hope is running low, the vessel that contains whole universes desperate to blind every soul on earth with its intensity.

The world has hardened the innocent — but not you, never you. You are a transcendent sort of miracle, the protector of your very own purity. By your logic, good conquers evil, always. The light never fails.

Spring

Spring is silent,

like the frosty winds

gradually evolving into

warm airs of bliss.

Spring is silent,

like the love I have for you,

quietly churning in my stomach,

afraid to tell you how I feel for fear

you may be afraid of the intensity,

immensity of it all.

If I uttered those three words,

would it make a difference?

Would flowers take root and sprout

in your heart at the thought

that you matter to someone?

Spring is silent,

but if you really pay attention,

all those colours are screaming for you

to notice them.

Peace

I hope those dreams you talk about

so relentlessly

come true,

whether it is now or when you are 70,

even though you believe you might not make it.

I picture you letting go

of the weight of the world

by the ocean,

vowing to no longer cope, but to yearn:

from now on, the saltwater will guide you home.

And I know that you will not mind staying there

all on your own

but still, I hope he comes back for you.

Revival

In a trance, a dance, one that only soul lovers partake in. The beat of your heart against my palm like a gentle fist, the strands of springtime in my scalp. All of this earth is buzzing with life and you have set my stem alight without the matchsticks borne of the sun. Skin holes soaking in heat, the light no longer timid, no longer weeping in defeat. We have been revived, second chance, far from the rot that clogged the organs of our ill-polluted lives.

June

June arrives,

the blooming flowers a testament

to all we endured in the winter.

The sun shines on every forgotten corner,

screaming:

'Though you are dark you can still be loved!'

The lingering scent of daffodils lace the air

and now,

I believe in true love.

Sprouting

These polluted skin strands I finally unclasp, abandon my weaponry (only for you). My edges have yet to be blunt but I pull the weeds out from my heart and relent to just a sliver of affection.

This is the art of making a stranger yours.

Clawing your way into depths of dark material simply to yank the light out of decaying phantom hands, blind the shadow-accustomed spots with sun. The pleasurable fingernail digging into skin, a promise to stay, for to abandon is to betray. The slow but sure chipping away at my eggshell exterior, the exact temperature at melting point that makes you realise this fortress was a futile sort of armour anyway, the assembling of troops a mere performance, for I was never well-equipped to participate in this battle of indifference.

My want for affection intensifies at the feel of your flower-watering palms, and I feel the beginnings of a rose take root in the soil, you the sunlight that has reshaped me, remade me.

Stars

The branches of your veins are laced with gold,

my limbs glittered with the stuff of yours,

so when our fingertips intertwine,

I am made better,

my body replenished with light.

Heartbeat erratic,

pounding against the shrilling splitting of Jupiter.

Just for a second,

I can see the stars align in my peripheral.

Soon it will be dawn

This is my view of the fields at nightfall.

It is dark and there are no stars in the sky,

there is just the moon,

its light illuminating your face

in a way I appreciate.

This would be quite an eerie sight,

were it not for the red rose petals

swaying in the pitch black night,

an inaudible sort of music,

proof that there is beauty in the uncertain.

We cannot see ahead of us,

but do not be defeated:

soon it will be dawn.

A Brief Intermission for Love Notes

'You are part of my existence, part of myself. You have been in every line I have ever read.' – *Charles Dickens, Great Expectations*

I did not want to be held, caressed, repulsive, natural born sceptic.

I could only be the thing that kept you up at night, I was never made to be a lullaby, a nursery rhyme. I do not bloom like a flower but instead I sprout through the soil like a starved crop, greedy to kidnap the sun to refute scientific hope, to dissect my soul and seek out where the rot lies, and why it has infiltrated. I did not anticipate to enchant with this mess, I was not prepared for the unpacking of your suitcase, not at the sight of my distress, my inability to nurture a good thing. But I have not prepared a speech, and my mask has come undone this time.

This is me and yet you still believe there is something worth salvaging. How terrifying.

<u>Eyes speak the language of the soul.</u>

The desire to unravel

every piece of it,

every fabric

that makes mine the stuff of yours.

When you uncover me with your gaze,

prying every secret out of my fingers

with so much ease and precision,

you know that I cannot look away,

I cannot help but surrender.

Because that hue of your irises

has been the waves causing shipwrecks.

It is the storm amongst the winds,

and it is that same indigo

which will provoke

unspeakable chaos within me.

We have said everything without saying a word.

Now, I cannot help drowning

in your demanding oceans,

and you have not been kind enough

to throw me a life jacket.

Ecstatic, tearing through evergreen forests. Beauty in terror, beauty *is* terror, but one that sustains you, that dilutes itself into necessary passion. Longing across the room, grazes of fingertips in passing, a common language foreign to the rest. Lost in a trance, a dance, where the music never stops playing, where each season is accompanied by melody.

Threading our fingers together, home, home is the heartbeat that thrums alongside yours, that always pumps in synchrony. Our own definition of it, each atom bound together, wound together in a way that makes it impossible to come apart. My missing rib.

Moments of darkness, when I should have remembered that yes, they are out there.

The people that could save us, the people that we are lonely for. Now, moments of recklessness, chaos, but in a way that feels safe, that cradles us.

All this love has hands to hold now.

The wet soil sticks to my legs, and instead of lying in it and letting the dirt consume me, I brush it off my knees. Flowers sprout at the mere sound of your voice, like a hymn restoring their faith in life.

We abandon the darkness of the shade under the meadow trees for lighter adventures, palms entwined as the sun caresses our yielding skin. We dart through the woods to reach the brightness at the end of the clearing. Once I had abandoned all hope, but now one look at you is enough to grant me unwavering strength.

All of this pain *softened*, sweetened by the honey in the thriving space. Amidst the unnerving hum of beekeepers and the sting that derives from the coffin of sufferings untold, there is you, bridging the gap between solitude and comfort, the gentle caress of the wind accumulated within your *weakening* fingertips.

I have remoulded the shape of my clay only to fit snugly under your frame, against the chest that so rises and falls like a sun frozen, frostbitten, unwilling to see another day and yet attempting to anyway.

This is not patchwork threaded by the strings of fate – I willed our paths to intersect, drilled down the groundwork for the gravel way by hand, angles and diagonals scribbled down furiously on tea-watered maps.

You were the sweetness necessary to acquire, and I set myself the goal of prying open the inner mechanisms of your soul.

After all, a wish only exists to be granted.

All I have is yours.

Cherry picking, anger dissolved

Flower petals absolved of premature sin

Into the Light

Gardens no longer untended

The sun does not shun

Weeds untangled, discarded, Our Father

Hope

I catch a glimpse of hope and I reach out and snatch it, fingers gripping, teeth gritting. I untangle myself from any thought that tells me I do not deserve to retrieve my glow back. Because here I am.

I have made it to July, comforting sun and flowers sprouting in full splendour.

I open up the windows so that the stench of winter and disappointment drift away into a hole that will never widen again. The bugs no longer bite into the peaches I pick: they have found more sour things to infiltrate. **No petal is dry, no fruit unripe.** No hope is a lie, because I see how it grows here right inside of my palm. I feel that God has and will continue to watch over me forever.

The light within me has ignited and this time it will not waver, and it will not go out. I call out to the sun and let it enter.

All flowers need a mixture of sunlight and water to grow, though the amount varies. Sometimes we are afraid that if we enjoy basking in the light for too long it will be overshadowed by the clouds and taken away. Perhaps we need the devastating to grow. Perhaps we need to love without the fear of letting go.

New beginnings

I make my bed (not reluctantly),

I part the curtains to welcome in the light,

I sit on the kitchen counter

and sip my coffee,

milk and two sugars,

I take in what is in front of me now.

Past and future are foreign concepts,

and I dare to think that I am more

kind than vengeful.

Sun

The clouds part,

and the sun emerges.

It shines on me, mockingly,

chuckling in my face, smug.

Amused that I believed it would never rise again.

Arrival

Heat rush,

metamorphosis as the flower skins erupt.

Fountain water licking fingertips,

daffodil bits seeking shelter in the vein.

Heart flutters within ribcage,

a marigold's preferred place of resurrection.

Blooming out of doom,

the wilting halted within

the gaps of the tombstone.

Ascendency,

a tendency to gravitate towards the light.

Pomegranate pulp softened,

sugar packets unopened in the shimmer,

granules no longer rotten,

gnawed in the glow of the after.

None of this is violent,

for my fists unclench,

and I mimic the opening of petal heads.

Gently.

Recollection

Afternoon sun sitting, relishing, fingertip kissing, please do not slip through the fibres of my palms just yet, I want to be worthy of being kept. We might go numb soon, yet I cannot distrust you. All of this is picture perfect, desired portrait. Let us not do a disservice to our past selves. Think of infant you, never like this could we ever be kids, let us ingrain ourselves into the present moment.

August

August is announced.

Cherries are not savoured with unrestrained vigour now, for we have been trained, we are tamed. Now, there are napkins for our sins. The stains might remain but it is bright outside and the ecstasy survives.

Sun lust, a poppy bath in the light. The dandelion fuzz does not escape us. We squirm not, we do not flee far into the screams of the horizon.

Perhaps we have conquered fate, outsmarted decay, for I no longer weep in the bark of willow trees, I burst forth and sprout wings.

After all, wallowing in sorrow was never the answer, and I do not desire to sink into that which is barren any longer. We eradicate the filth from our fingertips and give ourselves over to a more cradling sort of bliss.

Magnolia

I've got a coral of magnolia in my pocket.

Do you think that will be enough to release

all the tension from your body?

Or can I get you to breathe

by laying you amidst

the bulbous begonia blossoms,

head tilted towards the sun?

Look at all the hues of the morning sky

If you can't see them, can you feel them?

Look at how bright the world is,

I need you to believe it.

Vibrancy

The water in the lake

is the same deep hue as your eyes:

I fear that I shall drown in it,

and so I scrap my plans of swimming.

To the left,

a hedge of strawberries get tangled up,

twisting and turning like snakes,

hungry for some undeserved meal.

The sun is a fiery amber,

it almost looks as if it could jump out of the sky.

See? Summer is not only peaceful calm,

but delirious passion too.

Sun II

The sun reflects on my skin

through the windowpanes,

and I feel calm.

It is surprising.

Am I awaiting a life-altering event?

Or will I finally experience a period of rest?

I expected to be bursting to the brim

with a range of emotions,

but instead I feel my fists unclench.

Pretty birds make their arrival known

and I let myself exhale,

after months of holding my breath.

Noodles

When you look at me,

you make *noodles* of my brain,

and I feel all my complexities

fall down the drain.

Brutal

Winter, I feel as if I may have judged you a bit too harshly. You are brutal and vindictive and cold, but then again, I understand how hard it is to be warm when no one appears to love you.

Fireworks

Hungry. Tongue against teeth, each glance void of delicacy. Consumer, consumption, regular customer. Words I never tire of saying, repeated acts of devotion. No love unrequited or heartless, no fingertips letting go after years of holding on. This will not rust. I refuse to speak, fear of jinxing. A dream or reality? Fog emerging from my peripheral, because how can a thing so beloved exist in so wretched a world?

Fireflies

You are a light in the darkness, fluorescent hues abnormally splendorous to the human eye. I had breathed in blue and black before you, no colours flowing through my veins.

But now I see in neon, rays buzzing with a kind of electricity that causes the air to fizzle, making it something to taste and touch, transcending human senses.

Would I have attached myself to you sooner had I known it was possible to be saved like this? Would I have followed where the fireflies lead? My lantern, my flashlight. A burning fire, one that cannot be supressed or hidden, winter a foreign concept. No icicles instead of bone, no more stone in place of heart, or spine frosted by sorrow.

Drawing me towards you slowly, pulling at the fibres of my very being. A promise that it is not too late to hope. Reassurance that God has not forsaken me.

The epitome of love

I look at you, and I ponder

Can I love you back, I wonder?

Do I have it in me?

But I utter my prayers and decide I am capable

Yes, I will shower you with hearts in abundance

I shall cherish the brightest sunshine

and offer you uncomfortable sacrifices

I know because I have been taught

Because what were we saved for, if not to love?

Was our saving not exactly that, an act of love?

We loved because He first loved us – 1 John 4:19

There is a light that never goes out

I promise I promise I promise,

that there is a light that refuses to go out,

forever unwavering.

This anguish will not last forever,

its size in your chest will decrease until it is

merely a weightless particle starved, not fed.

And then it will disintegrate.

Shatter

I shattered into a billion pieces

Nothing changed

I shattered into a billion pieces

Then the world shifted

I want to be happy alone

I never needed to be strong

Flowers

You, the flowers that make up all the gardens on Earth. My fingernails ache from all the oranges I peel for you, but this is what I was meant to do. The sun bleeds until it is an aching gold, and every surface of the universe shimmers. In this beautiful haze, your freckles are ultraviolet, and for a moment we exist in every possible colour. I feel as if my longing can only be satisfied by you, the length of it is endless. You are everything I have ever looked at, now I cannot turn away.

Hoping

The weary and tired hope,

hope that they can find a place on earth

that makes them feel oh so small,

so that they may not dwell on their troubles,

with the knowledge that

the stars weep before they fall asleep,

and the sun does not wish to rise,

but it still does anyway,

in spite of it all.

Fulfilling

You walk through the door and my petals are being watered again. My roots were so close to extinction, I was prepared for it, I did not want to bloom. And then, after severe dehydration, you came through like a flood mingled with sunshine. My legs cannot stand upright when you look at me like I am the only person ever. I think this can transcend eternity.

Longing

I dream of you in colours that

aren't visible to the human eye.

I cry to God in appreciation,

for He believed me worthy enough

to exist alongside His greatest creation.

I longed for you in the womb,

I longed for you as soon as I had a heartbeat.

Bouquet

I am a bouquet of all the best flowers.

A crimson rose full of deep desire, sometimes anger, but mostly passionate love for those I care deeply for.

A blue lilac, because when I feel sadness, I feel it to my core.

A sunflower, yellow at full brightness, golden hues of glitter, infecting everyone with my joy.

A white carnation, for I will never let the innocent child in me die - I carry her with me wherever I go.

A pink tulip. Sometimes I still visualise the world in rose colour, pretending that there is no wretched in anything or anyone, just like I used to do for most of my life.

I feel everything deeply. I am one thing at a time, and everything all at once too. And that is fine. Because though I feel the blue hues of life, I will never let them overpower my yellow. After all, there is always sunshine after even the darkest and loudest of storms.

There is always dawn after dusk.

Sincerely

This worry flows and ebbs within me.

It is like a tide,

once low, once impossible to tame.

But I know that it will level off over time.

I am no longer hesitant that the sun will rise,

and so I teach myself to smile,

and when I do, I teach myself to mean it.

Epilogue

I feel my fists unclench, bell jar lifting. How unrewarding is this pent up anger after all. Knot in chest untangling, air flowing in and out. Light, almost as if I were floating. But even if I am above the clouds, I will always come back to myself eventually. Head above water, all fears weighing me down sinking to the sea's bottom. Is it truly that easy to let go of it all? No, but then again, nothing ever is. The most important discovery is that the darkness was not meant to consume.

And maybe love does exist, somewhere, somehow, and maybe I believe because I feel so full of it. It is hidden, deep within my core, the sliver of hope that did not die when everything else did. All of it is waiting for you. The thing that your soul yearns for, the people you were born to hold. The things worth clinging onto, worth living for.

All you have to do is *look*.

Let the light in.

@prettypoemwriter

.

Printed in Great Britain
by Amazon